Welcome

Dear praying friends,

Last year, just after the 2014 prayer guide was ready for printing, Ron, the international coordinator for the 30 Days of Prayer for the Muslim World guide, went to be with the Lord. Ron's death was sudden and unexpected and a great loss to this prayer movement. We wanted to honor him at the of this 2015 edition for his commitment to loving Muslims through prayer, educating the Body of Christ about the Muslim world and how to pray for it.

Before he died, Ron had made arrangements for the 2015 edition to be organized around a series of articles by David Garrison, researcher and author of the book *A Wind in the House of Islam* (available at WorldChristian.com). David has generously shared content from his important and inspirational book with our readers for this special edition. We know that you will be encouraged as you read about the global impact of over 20 years of regular prayer for the Muslim world, prompted by the efforts of 30 Days International.

We (WorldChristian.com) want to also express our thanks to:

1 The new international volunteer coordinators in the UK who have stepped in to arrange the material for this year's prayer guide;
2 The many promoters, sponsors and distributors of the North American booklet editions, and of course;
3 To the many of you who participate regularly in faithful prayer.

Please also remember us and the other regional coordinators around the world who seek to mobilize the Body of Christ to pray with faith, hope and love for our world's Muslim neighbors.

Paul (for WorldChristian.com, the North American publisher of 30 Days)

...material are produced, published and distributed by coordinators in different language and geographic regions.

Our Sponsors Ministries and organizations whose advertising significantly contributes toward the North American edition of this prayer guide are featured starting on page 43. We hope that you will peruse those pages; they provide opportunities for further involvement.

Making A Donation Help us support ministry opportunities around the world by making a tax-deductible donation payable to: WorldChristian Concern, PO Box 9208, Colorado Springs CO 80932. You can also donate securely online at www.worldchristianconcern.org/donate

Additional Booklets See Order Form on page 56

Ramadan

This annual prayer guide is designed to be used during the Islamic month of Ramadan (an important 30-day period of Islamic observance). The dates for Ramadan follow an Islamic calendar, a slight variation of an astronomically based lunar calendar. In 2015, Ramadan will be from about June 18 through July 17. This will vary from region to region as the fasting period normally begins and ends with the sighting of the crescent moon. Although the starting year of the 30 Days International movement was 1993, our 2015 booklet is the 24th edition (because the Islamic year is shorter by about 11 days compared to the Gregorian calendar year). The Islamic calendar starts with the year 622 A.D. when Muhammad fled Mecca for Medina; the current year in the Islamic calendar is 1436. *Note: The moon is not an object of worship in Islam.*

Muslim Americans Snapshots from a 2011 Pew Research Center survey

The majority of Muslims in the USA (69%) profess that their religion is very important to their lives (equal to the percentage of Christians). This compares to 80% in regions such as sub-Sahara Africa, South and Southeast Asia, and 60% across North Africa and the Middle East, and only about 50% in formerly Communist dominated Muslims regions.

"Most Muslim Americans seem well-integrated into American society," and twice as many of them express satisfaction with the way life in the USA is going than the general public.

"Almost half of both U.S. Muslims and U.S. Christians report attending worship services at least weekly."

"Nearly half of Muslim Americans believe that Muslim leaders have not done enough to speak out against extremists."

"While a majority of U.S. Muslims say that it is more difficult to be a Muslim in the U.S. since 9/11, most think the American people are generally friendly or neutral toward Muslim Americans."

The daily activities of Muslim Americans look very similar to those of the general public. For example 58% watch at least an hour of TV nighty (compared to 62%), 57% use social networking sites (compared to 44%), 44% display the American flag (compared to 59%), and 48% watch pro or college sports (compared to 47%).

In many respects U.S. Muslims resemble fellow Americans more than Muslims around the world. They are less observant of Islamic practices, consider Islam open to different interpretations (57% think so, compared to a global median of 27%), and half of them even report having best friends who are not Muslims.

Most sources put the number of Muslim Americans at around three million.

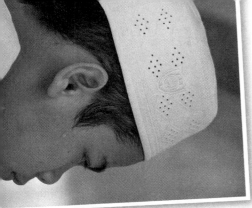

Islam

According to Muslims, Islam began with the very first human beings, Adam and Eve, who were supposed to submit themselves to God. The word Islam means submission. Muslims believe that Islam is the true universal monotheistic religion revealed to mankind through prophets such as Abraham, Moses, David and Jesus. Their teaching however is believed to have been distorted, and was, according to Islamic beliefs, succeeded by the last prophet, Muhammad, to whom the One Supreme God revealed a superior message that is recorded in the Qur'an and venerated as the verbatim Word of God.

No one can possibly understand Islam without knowing something about the life of Muhammad who is revered by all Muslims. He is considered the "ideal man," a model for all Muslims, but is in no way to be seen as divine, nor is he worshipped. No images of Muhammad are permitted (in order to prevent idolatry).

The prophet of Islam was born in 570 AD in Mecca, a city in Saudi Arabia. His father died before he was born, and after his mother died when he was six, and his grandfather when he was eight, he was raised by an uncle. He married when he was 25 and was for much of his life until age 40 involved in caravan-trading ventures. While during much of Muhammad's lifetime idol worship was common among the tribes of Arabia (with Mecca being a center that housed an estimated 360 gods), Muhammad became influenced through contacts with Jews and Christians and certain other Arabs to embrace a monotheistic outlook.

According to Muslim history, at the age of 40, in 610 AD, Muhammad began to receive revelations and instruction that he believed were from the archangel Gabriel. These "revelations" which Muhammad proclaimed as the the final and superior message from the One Supreme God form the basis of the Qur'an. Over the next two decades he developed a following and eventually an army that allowed him to to subdue opposition and ban the worship of idols. Muhammad died of natural causes in 632 AD in Medina, Saudi Arabia. Disputes over his succession led to the formation of the two main branches of Islam, Sunni and Shia.

The five pillars

The Islamic religion is lived out according to five main "pillars" which are obligatory religious practices for all adult Muslims:

1 **Reciting the Creed (shahada)** "There is no God but Allah and Mohammed is his prophet."
2 **Prayer (salat)** Five times each day.
3 **Almsgiving (zakat)** Both obligatory and voluntary giving to the poor.
4 **Fasting (saum)** Especially during the "holy" month of Ramadan.
5 **Pilgrimage (hajj)** At least once in a lifetime to Mecca, known as the Hajj.

30 Days of Prayer for the Muslim World
Encouraging, educating and enabling since 1993

Though the issues faced by the Muslim world change from year to year, the aim of the *30 Days of Prayer for the Muslim World* prayer guide remains to encourage, educate and enable. Through prayer, we engage in an act of love for Muslim people around the world — sharing their burdens, understanding their concerns and petitioning God to help them. In this way, we fulfill the command of Jesus to love our neighbors.

Encouraging
30 Days International began with a group of people who felt compelled to change the way they understood the Muslim world and to see them in the same way God does — as unique individuals, families and tribes. Readers are encouraged to pray for that same inspiration and let God direct their prayers with His loving knowledge of the Muslim world.

Educating
With more information at our disposal than ever before, it is necessary to use discernment in how we form our understanding about the world around us. This guide draws its information about the Muslim world primarily from people who live or have lived among Muslims with the aim of loving and blessing them. We try to echo their voices and hope to help our readers recognize the diversity that exists in culture and theology within the Muslim world.

Enabling
Praying during Ramadan is a helpful way for Christians to identify with Muslims. During this time, many Muslims are seeking encounters with God and a better understanding of His ways. Each year, we receive reports that this is what God does — for both Muslims and the Christians who pray for them. This is a perfect time to talk to Muslim friends about what God is revealing to you, and to share with other Christians what you are learning as you pray.

To learn more about Islam — the religion, the history, etc., we encourage you to peruse the many books on the subject available at WorldChristian.com.

> Through prayer, we engage in an act of love for Muslim people around the world

Where are our prayers taking us?

The numbers on the map indicate the page where you will find a prayer article about that area of the world.

DID YOU KNOW?

23.2% of the global population identify as Muslim — that's 1.6 billion people.

62% of these people live in the Asia–Pacific region.

20% in the Middle East and North Africa.

16% in sub-Saharan Africa.

3% in Europe.

Less than 1% of the global Muslim population lives in North America, Latin America and the Caribbean.

(Pew Research Center, December 2012)

Nine Rooms in the House of Islam

This year, the prayer guide is structured around a newly published book by David Garrison called *A Wind in the House of Islam*. The book explores nine geocultural areas of Muslim identity — described as "Rooms in the House of Islam" — where there are movements of people turning to faith in Jesus. The nine Rooms are explained in the pages of this guide, with further opportunities for prayer.

Turkestan

North Africa

Persian World

Arab World

Western South Asia

West Africa

Eastern South Asia

East Africa

Indo-Malaysia

An unprecedented turning

> we are seeing the greatest and most wide-reaching turning of Muslims to Christ in history

For nearly 14 centuries, Islam and Christianity have been engaged in a spiritual contest for the souls of millions. For over 12 of those centuries, Islam has been the clear victor. Since Muhammad founded Islam in AD 622, millions of Christians have been swept into the House of Islam — the name Muslims give to their global religious empire.

But what about the opposite? Have there been movements of at least 1,000 people turning from Islam and being baptized? Not until recently. During the first 350 years of Islam's history, while Christian populations from the Middle East to Spain were being conquered and converted by Islamic armies, there was only one movement in the other direction. In 982, history records that 12,000 Arab Muslim men sought baptism. Two more movements took place in the 12th and 13th centuries in what is today Lebanon and Libya, respectively. In the next six centuries there was not a single such movement to Christ among Muslims.

Then in 1870, on the remote island of Java, the first modern-day movement of Muslims to Christ occurred, followed by a second movement in Ethiopia from 1890–1920. Not until 1967 do we begin to see another movement, this time of more than two million Muslims, again in Indonesia, who were baptized into hundreds of Christian churches.

In the last two decades of the 20th century, however, the tide began to turn. Movements broke out in Algeria, Soviet Central Asia, Bangladesh, and Iran. In the first 14 years of the 21st century, new Muslim movements to Christ have erupted across the Muslim world, from West Africa to Indonesia and everywhere in between. The 21st century alone has seen the addition of 69 new Muslim movements to Christ. In our day, we are seeing the greatest and most wide-reaching turning of Muslims to Christ in history.

HOW CAN WE PRAY?

- *The current wave of Muslim movements to Christ has happened at the same time as an increase in prayer for the Muslim world. It's no coincidence that the 30 Days Prayer movement has just commemorated its 23rd year. Pray that the Spirit of God will continue to sweep through the Muslim world, drawing Islam's millions to realize their need for salvation in Christ alone!*

Afghanistan: If you seek, you will find!

Discipleship is a difficult and dangerous challenge in a nation where identifying as a follower of Jesus can make you a target for extremist violence. However, one believer in Afghanistan shares this story about how determined seekers are finding what they're looking for:

"I met one of our young believers through a social media site. I was very cautious about meeting with him face to face, but I accidentally sent him my cell phone number. He kept calling me, day and night, asking to meet me and for copies of the New Testament. So I prayed about it and agreed to meet him. I said goodbye to my family and kissed the children. I drove to his part of the city along with another young believer, and parked the car far from the place he was waiting. I told my friend, 'If you don't hear from me in ten minutes, drive the car and all of you get out of the city immediately.'

"When I met this brother, he gave me a big hug and was very happy to see me … but honestly when he was trying to come closer I was still thinking of how to get away! But he reassured me, so I gave him the two New Testaments and he was thrilled. He had found what he'd been wanting for a long time. The next day, we met again and he shared his story with me …

"He was seeking for Jesus and couldn't find anyone in the city where he lives. So he decided to save some money and buy a second-hand computer. He borrowed an Internet connection, taught himself to use email and social media and started searching for other believers in our nation. He found me despite all those challenges! He's so excited to learn about Jesus and so is his family, and he is sharing his understanding with others. God does His work in ways we don't understand sometimes, but we give Him glory!"

HOW CAN WE PRAY?

- *Pray for those in Afghanistan who are seeking to understand more about Jesus, that doors will open for them to find the teachings of Christ.*
- *Pray for peace in this nation and the freedom to worship and pursue God.*
- *Pray for the safety and encouragement of those who believe in secret.*

Nine Rooms in the House of Islam

If we are going to pray effectively for the Muslim world, we must see the Muslim world as it sees itself, and as it is. The eighth-century Muslim jurist Abu Hanifa (AD 699–767) divided the world into two houses: the House of Islam (Arabic *Dar al-Islam*) and the House of War (*Dar al-Harb*). The House of Islam indicated those nations where Muslims were the dominant population and Islamic law guided the populace into Islamic submission. The House of War constituted those lands where Muslims were in the minority — where Islam was not yet dominant.

The House of Islam, with its 1.6 billion adherents, is anything but a uniform whole. It's as diverse as the Christian religion. Muslims in West Africa hold very different cultural, linguistic and worldview perspectives from those in Iran, Bangladesh or Indonesia. To pray more intelligently for the Muslim world, we need to see it in all of its cultural diversity.

The House of Islam can be divided geoculturally into nine distinct regions or "Rooms." These nine Rooms are: (1) West Africa, (2) North Africa, (3) Eastern Africa, (4) the Arab World, (5) the Persian World, (6) Turkestan, (7) Western South Asia, (8) Eastern South Asia, and (9) Indo-Malaysia.

West Africa and Eastern Africa are filled with Muslims from largely animistic tribal backgrounds. The Arab world, where Islam originated, was previously Christian and home to many of Christianity's earliest Church Fathers. The Persian world was predominantly Zoroastrian before its seventh-century conquest by Islamic armies. Central Asian Turkestan was the home of shamanistic Turko-Mongolian tribes with scattered communities of Nestorian Christians before Tamerlane and the Golden Horde eradicated them in the 14th–16th centuries. These same Turkic conquerors subdued the peoples of what is today Afghanistan, Pakistan and western India in the centuries that followed. Islam's advance eastward toppled Hindu and Buddhist kingdoms in what is today eastern India, Bangladesh and western Myanmar. By the 13th century, Islam had already gained a foothold in the Indonesia archipelago, gradually converting the Hindu spiritualism of what is today Malaysia and the largest Muslim country, Indonesia.

HOW CAN WE PRAY?

● *Pray for each of the nine Rooms in the House of Islam by name. Ask God to pour out His Spirit on the Muslims of these Rooms, making them aware of their need for salvation in the person of Jesus Christ.*

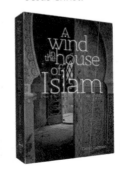

David Garrison
A Wind in the House of Islam

Available at
WorldChristian.com

The University of Dhaka, Bangladesh

The University of Dhaka is the oldest and largest university in Bangladesh. Established in 1921, it gained a reputation as the "Oxford of the East" during its early years. It hosts a wide variety of institutes and departments of various disciplines, and has more than 38,000 students and

over 3,000 staff members. The university motto is "Truth will prevail!"

One elderly professor enjoys taking visitors to the front steps of the Arts building, where a large monument featuring two men and a woman in heroic advance reminds the visitor that the University of Dhaka has been a significant contributor to the modern history of Bangladesh. After the partition of India, it became the centre of progressive and democratic movements. "We will continue this tradition," the professor assures.

In recent years, a small department called the Department for World Religions and Culture has been established. Lecturers are not the only

teachers in these classes; believers of these religions are invited to teach as well. This gives an opportunity for Christians, a small minority of 0.5%, to be heard in Bangladesh society. They are able to teach the entire gospel and tell stories about Jesus Christ. About 300 students are able to read sections of the Bible and learn about the Good News each year. The department favors dialog, but not syncretism. They say, "We need to know each other's faith well in order to respect the beliefs of a fellow human!"

> " They are able to teach the entire gospel and tell stories about Jesus Christ "

HOW CAN WE PRAY?

- That the Department for World Religions and Culture would continue in its open-mindedness.
- That the students' hearts and minds will be open and that the motto of the university — "Truth will prevail!" — will become a reality.
- That God will guide the Christian lecturers and professors in their teaching.

West Africa: A tale of two oceans

West Africa is the tale of two oceans: the Atlantic to the west and the great Sahara Desert to the north. These oceans provided access to the region's more than 300 million inhabitants. Europeans began arriving from the Atlantic in the 15th century to stake out trading posts from which they would gather slaves and gold, eventually building colonies from what is today Mauritania in the north to Nigeria in the south. The other ocean, the Sahara Desert, one that we often fail to see, had already provided passage for northern conquerors centuries earlier. As early as the eighth century the Sahara yielded passage to Arab and Berber invaders from North Africa on camel caravans, rightly called "ships of the desert," seeking the same prizes — slaves, ivory and gold — while leaving behind their Islamic faith.

In the 1960s, independence movements swept West Africa, but the older conflict between Christian and Muslim communities increased. Today, West Africa is divided between Muslim populations in the north and east and Christian populations along the southern and western Atlantic coastal zone.

The earlier allure of slaves, ivory and gold has been supplanted by other attractions, such as the diamonds that led to genocidal wars in Sierra Leone and Liberia (1980–2002) and the rich oil fields that have generated both wealth and conflict in Nigeria.

Christianity has grown rapidly in West Africa over the past century, and much of the region's wealth has been under the control of Christian communities living near the coasts. Muslims in the arid interior have seen their fortunes deteriorate as global warming and the expanding Sahara have depleted agricultural and grazing lands. The result is an increasingly impoverished and desperate Islamic populace, giving rise to militant responses from groups such as Boko Haram, Ansaru, and the Movement for Oneness and Jihad in West Africa.

HOW CAN WE PRAY?

- Pray for the dozens of emerging Islamic movements to Christ in West Africa.
- Pray for the physical as well as spiritual needs of the Muslim population in West Africa.
- Pray for God to protect West Africans from the assault of Islamic militant groups.

WEST AFRICA	
Nations	22
Muslim people groups	514
Total population	335,556,076
Muslim population	105,239,092

The people of north Mali

The north of Mali is a huge sandpit — the southern Sahara. This area is known for the Tuareg in their blue robes, riding on camels. Lesser known are the Songhai, who live along the Niger river in north-east Mali, mainly in the cities of Gao and Timbuktu. From the mid-15th to the late 16th centuries, the Songhai Empire was one of the largest Islamic empires in history. This area is still largely unreached by the gospel — 99 per cent are Muslims, and there are very few Christians.

Tamasheq and Songhai are the two major languages spoken in north Mali. The New Testament has been available in Tamasheq for a few years now, but the Songhai version was only just distributed and dedicated to the population in January 2015. The Word of God in these languages is the key to the people's hearts.

The ongoing conflict and rise of extremism as a result of rebellions in 2012 and 2013 has caused many of the population to become disillusioned with Islam. This has created a great openness to faith in Jesus, but there are so few workers to address the enormous physical and spiritual needs of this region.

Fatima has a crippled foot because of polio. Over the years, she has become open to know more about Jesus and has even helped in translating the Bible. However, she does not dare to openly confess her faith in Jesus because of the fear of expulsion from her family. This is true of many others in north Mali.

HOW CAN WE PRAY?

- *Pray for peace in the ongoing conflict over this region.*
- *Pray for opportunities for more people in north Mali to understand the message of Christ and its power to transform and bring peace.*
- *Pray for more Christian workers who can demonstrate the love of Jesus in this area.*

North Africa: The faith of our fathers

For centuries North Africa was a Christian heartland that produced some of Christianity's greatest Church leaders. Augustine, Tertullian, Cyprian, Perpetua and Felicitas have inspired and informed generations of Christians right up to the present day. Despite this great legacy, the arrival of Islam in the seventh century marked the beginning of the end of one of Christianity's greatest strongholds. By the 12th century, with the invasion of Arab Bedouin tribes, indigenous Christianity was all but eradicated. Today, the North African nations stretching from Mauritania to Libya claim to be 99 percent Islamic: but something is changing.

North Africa is historically the land of the Berber — aboriginal mountain peoples who have seen centuries of invaders come and go. Much of the population today is a blend of Berber and Arab culture that has been on the forefront of centuries-long conflict between the House of Islam and the West.

Rafiq was one of the millions of Berbers who left his North African homeland seeking a better life in Europe. He regarded himself as more European than Muslim. A talented musician and composer, Rafiq — for reasons unknown to him — chose the life of Jesus as the subject of a musical he was writing. Immersing himself in the Gospels, Rafiq became a follower of Jesus.

Taking his new faith back to North Africa, Rafiq found himself in the midst of a turning of thousands of his Berber compatriots who had also discovered what their ancestor, Augustine, had written about 15 centuries earlier: "The soul cannot rest, until it finds its rest in Thee." One Muslim-background Christ follower confessed, "Our ancestors were followers of Jesus. Augustine was a Berber like us. We are just returning to the faith of our fathers."

HOW CAN WE PRAY?

- Pray for the emerging movements in North Africa.
- Pray for the satellite television and radio ministries that have contributed to these movements.
- Pray for the Christian families in North Africa that seek to raise their children as believers in the face of strong opposition.

> " the North African nations stretching from Mauritania to Libya claim to be 99 percent Islamic: but something is changing "

NORTH AFRICA	
Nations	6
Muslim people groups	82
Total population	100,631,350
Muslim population	99,029,643

Chad: Opportunity in the heart of Africa

Musa lives with his extended family in a small village in Chad. He is in the first year at school and shares his teacher and classroom with 210 other students. Most of the time he has to sit on the ground because there are not enough benches. Unfortunately, Musa's teacher speaks to him in French, a language that he doesn't understand very well — he speaks Chadian Arabic.

Many days, Musa and his friends go to school in vain because his teacher does not show up. When the teacher is there, however, they spend most of the time repeating what the teacher says. While Musa is good about memorizing his lessons, he doesn't always understand what he is repeating. Will he leave the primary school, like most Chadian children, without ever having learned actually to read or write?

Musa's cousin, Abdallah, lives in another village. Abdallah's father is the imam of their village. His many children and their education are important to him, but public schools in the area failed to meet his standards. So he asked a Christian worker to come and start a school for his children. Abdallah loves his school. He is one student among 20 (his siblings and a few neighborhood kids who can afford the private school fees). His teacher is able to instruct in both French and Chadian Arabic. He also enjoys listening to the Bible stories that the teacher tells them every morning. It is so different from reciting without understanding!

The catastrophic situation of Chad's public educational system has led Muslims throughout the country to ask for Christian schools for their children, welcoming a good education for their children as part of the blessings of the kingdom of God.

HOW CAN WE PRAY?

- *For more good educational opportunities for the children of Chad.*
- *That teachers will have wisdom and courage as they teach and demonstrate the message of Christ.*
- *That the seed of God's Word will grow and bear fruit and that many families will come to follow Jesus.*

Eastern Africa: A Macedonian call

Like West Africa, the 357 million people of Eastern Africa have been exploited by both Muslim and Christian invaders; Christian and Muslim groups have been embroiled in conflict for generations.

Islam first arrived in East Africa in AD 614, when a group of Muslim refugees, sent by the Prophet Muhammad, sought asylum from persecution by his own Quraysh tribe. This Islamic foothold expanded in the centuries that followed until Islam became the dominant religion in the region for the next thousand years. But things are changing.

Elias was an East African missionary living in the crowded Somali refugee camps of a large city in the Horn of Africa. One night he was startled by the unexpected arrival of a Somali sheikh named Abdul-Ahad. Elias wondered if this would be the night that Somali militant group Al-Shabaab would choose to extract their revenge on yet another Christian.

> Christian and Muslim groups have been embroiled in conflict for generations

As Elias opened the door, the sheikh abruptly demanded, "Yes or No. Jesus' blood paid for the sins of everyone?"

Elias nervously replied, "Yes."

The sheikh responded adamantly, "You're lying!" Then he hesitated before saying, "The blood of Jesus cannot forgive my sins."

Abdul-Ahad told Elias of the violence he'd committed in war-torn Mogadishu. The old sheikh began to tremble and weep. "I need relief from that," he said.

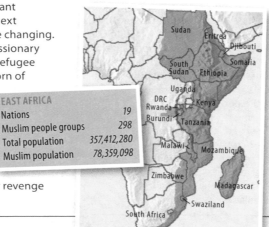

EAST AFRICA

Nations	19
Muslim people groups	298
Total population	357,412,280
Muslim population	78,359,098

Elias told him, "If you and I agree tonight, then God will forgive you."

The old sheikh prayed with Elias, and Abdul-Ahad was saved that night. Before he left, he turned to Elias and said to him, "When you look at me on the street, you see my Muslim hat and my beard, and you are afraid of me. But you need to know that inside we are empty. Don't be afraid of us. We need the gospel."

"That was my Macedonian call," Elias said. "I have never forgotten it."

HOW CAN WE PRAY?

- *Pray that more of the millions of Christians in Eastern Africa will embrace the Macedonian call to their Muslim neighbors.*
- *Pray for Muslims in war-torn Somalia and neighboring lands to find peace and freedom in the gospel of Jesus Christ.*
- *Pray that God would protect the emerging movements of Muslims to Christ in the Eastern Africa Room in the House of Islam.*

The Orma and Wardei of East Africa

> The lives of the Orma and Wardei tribes call to mind John 10:14–16, where Jesus calls himself the Good Shepherd.

One local worker writes: "When the sun goes down, I watch the Orma bring their animals into their village. First, the little boys pass with the goats and sheep, then the men with the cows. When they reach the village, the sounds of the animals mix with the voices of children singing and the sound of drums. There is joy when the animals return — the herder knows every animal, and they know the herder. The animals know the way, but sometimes one is missing and the herder returns into the bush, calling out 'Oi! Oi! Oi!' until he finds it. If he doesn't find it, other family members join in the search the next day."

The Wardei have similar lifestyles to the Orma; they live in the Tana Delta region of Kenya. Their estimated population is 53,000. There is little information about them, and few agencies are specifically reaching out to them. They are isolated from other people groups, though some have intermarried with the Orma. Those from other tribes who come to their village usually do casual labor for them. The Wardei women normally build their house, as well as collect firewood, cook, sell milk, fetch water and care for the small calves. The men look after the cattle and move around with them in search of pasture. They follow Islam and some take more than one wife, especially those with a leading position in the village.

The chewing of *miraa (khat)* is common among Wardei men. *Miraa* is from a plant grown in the region and acts like a drug. It's big business and is also exported to Europe.

Tradition says that the Wardei originate from the Orma and were taken captive by the Somali for four generations. They returned to Kenya when it gained independence. That could explain why they speak Somali and not Orma. These tribes share history — let's pray that they find a future that includes the Good Shepherd.

HOW CAN WE PRAY?

- *Pray that the tribes would find the one true Shepherd.*
- *Pray that those addicted to* miraa *would find release from their addiction and the drugs trade.*
- *Pray that other believers will bring the news of the Shepherd who lays down His life for His sheep to the Orma and the Wardei.*

The Arab World: I know where I'm going

The Arab World is the central Room in the House of Islam. It's an amalgam of races and nationalities that bear testament to the legacy of seventh-century Arab Muslim conquerors. Today, the Arab League stretches across 22 member nations, and its speakers comprise the fourth or fifth largest language group in the world. Satellite TV or radio programs and the witness of both missionaries and ancient Christians are enabling many Arab Muslims to hear the gospel message, but the Holy Spirit is leading the way in convicting Arab Muslims of their need for a Savior. One such is a 58-year-old retired businessman named Mahad.

Since coming to faith, Mahad has brought members of 70 households to Christ, and leads a network of secret believers in Bible study and worship. The turning point for Mahad had been when his beloved wife died and he became depressed. This led to heart problems and eventually the need for open-heart surgery.

"The doctors told me my chances of survival were no better than five percent. As I went under the anesthesia, I prayed but felt no peace. As I was losing consciousness, I called out, 'Jesus,' three times.

"Immediately, I felt peace. While under the anesthesia, I had a vision of Jesus and my wife, together in a beautiful meadow. They both looked so happy. I felt such joy. I knew that in the real world I must have died, but that was all right; I was going to be with them. I moved closer, but then started falling away, but I didn't want to go back.

"I'll never forget that vision. The surgery was successful, but since that day my heart has been tied to Jesus. Before the surgery, I was afraid of dying. But now I know I will go to be with my wife and Jesus. My wife always loved Jesus. She never talked to me about it, but she always wanted Him close."

He held up a plaster figurine of Da Vinci's *Last Supper*, the kind sold to tourists in the market. "She bought this many years ago. When we get to heaven, we will ask her about it."

HOW CAN WE PRAY?

- *Pray that inhabitants of the homeland of the Bible would return to the faith of the Bible.*
- *Pray for God to protect new Arab Muslim-background believers from the persecution they face for following Christ.*
- *Pray for the millions of Arab Muslims who have yet to hear the good news of Jesus Christ.*

THE HOUSE OF ISLAM'S CENTRAL ROOM

ARAB WORLD	
Nations	21
Muslim people groups	240
Total population	236,992,225
Muslim population	204,473,439

Egypt: The leader of an underground church shares

In January 2014, Egypt drafted a new constitution. Article 1 declared Egypt an Islamic State; Article 2 established Islam as the state religion and *sharia* (Islamic law) as "the source of legislation" for the country.

Although the constitution protects the rights of religious minorities (Christians, Jews) better than former constitutions in Egypt, there is not complete freedom of religion. It is still considered illegal to convert to a different belief.

Bolos is leading a Christian underground organization in his homeland, Egypt:

"On the one hand Christians in Egypt are filled with joy and sense a deep love for their fellow men; on the other they have to fear for their lives because they have left Islam and are considered apostates. Yet, they are a testimony for Jesus through the love they show to their relatives and acquaintances. This love has already moved entire families to believe in the living God.

"… it's a risky ministry because we don't have the freedom of faith that other nations enjoy. We are working underground because in Egypt it is dangerous to tell Muslims about Jesus. There is not only danger from the government, but it is also unacceptable in Egyptian society.

"Egyptians who have found faith in Jesus are eager to pass on the love they have found to other Egyptians. We support them through training and networking. Or we help them to establish a small business of their own like a taxi-service so they can be financially independent if they have to break away from their Muslim communities.

"We also work in medical services, giving the poor free check-ups and urgently needed medicines. We try to be as wise as possible. Our focus is always on friendship, not on discussions or arguments. Our Muslim neighbors see the way we act. When they start asking questions we tell them about the love of God.

"I wish with all my heart that thousands, even millions, of Egyptian Muslims will find living faith in Jesus and become witnesses of their faith wherever they live. God's kingdom is being built here in Egypt."

HOW CAN WE PRAY?

- *That the families of new Egyptian believers will also come to know Christ.*
- *That more house churches will start through Muslim families deciding to believe in Jesus.*
- *That God would encourage Egyptian believers to remain strong and give them words and wisdom to reach their neighbors.*

The Persian World: How I see Him

Since the rise of the Ayatollah's Islamic Republic in 1979, the nearly 100 million Shi'ite Muslims of Iran have been identified to the West as members of the "axis of evil" in our world. But there is another story unfolding in the Persian Room in the House of Islam, a story of redemption and rebirth.

Since the Ayatollah's rise to power, hundreds of thousands of Iranian refugees have fled to other countries around the world. Everywhere they have gone, new house churches of Iranian Muslim-background followers of Jesus Christ have taken root. Over the past two decades, God has used what man intended for evil to bring about His good. Economic collapse, rampant drug addiction, ruinous wars with Iraq and the West, coupled with the bold witness of believers have drawn thousands of Iranians to faith in Jesus Christ.

Nadia and her family fled from Iran two years ago and were warmly welcomed by the Christian community in their new home country. She and her husband attended a Christian marriage weekend for Iranian-background immigrants designed to help Muslim-background couples re-establish their marriages on Christian principles, and move towards a Christian understanding of love between a husband and wife.

One of the exercises was for a husband to express his love to his wife. Nadia's husband volunteered. He took Nadia by the hand and in front of the whole group he told her boldly, 'Nadia, I love you,' and then kissed her publicly.

Nadia recalls the event and blushes: "That was the first time in our marriage that my husband told me that he loved me."

Shortly afterwards, Nadia's husband died unexpectedly. When asked how she could cope with the pain and loss, she replied, "Jesus' promise has helped me cope, the one where He said, 'Come to me, all you who are weary and burdened, and I will give you rest.' Jesus has carried me. Jesus has given me peace."

> " Jesus has carried me. Jesus has given me an unnatural peace. "

HOW CAN WE PRAY?

- Pray that Iran's leaders do not lead the millions of people in their country to utter destruction.
- Pray for the thousands of Persians coming to faith in Christ, that they would grow deep and wide in Christ.
- Pray that Christians in the West would replace hate and fear of Iran with love and compassion.

PERSIAN WORLD	
Nations	3
Muslim people groups	105
Total population	99,009,985
Muslim population	97,957,533

Peacemaking with Muslims?

Following the Prince of Peace demands it!

Rick Love, PhD

Together, Muslims and Christians comprise over half of the world's population

I taught a course on 'Peacemaking as God's Mission' at Denver Seminary last June. John, one of my students from Kenya, told the chilling story of the terrorist group, Al-Shabaab. Originally from Somalia, Al-Shabaab has begun infiltrating the mosques in Kenya, seeking to overthrow the government. John seemed overwhelmed by Al-Shabaab's brazen, evil plans. I struggled to answer, but then sensed God's guidance:

"First, you are not responsible to figure out how to stop Al-Shabaab, John. You are responsible to work for peace where God has placed you. God has given you a sphere of influence. Begin there. Encourage Christians to reach out in love to Muslims."

Second, I said, "John, you need to find noble Muslim peacemakers. You should partner with them to win the hearts and minds of their fellow Muslims and turn them against Al-Shabaab."

My response highlights two keys that will help us counter violent extremism and pursue peace with Muslims.

1. Peace begins with me. What does God expect of me in my sphere of influence?

Jesus said His children will be peacemakers (Matthew 5:9). Paul said that peacemaking is comprehensive in scope: "If possible, so far as it depends on you, live at peace with everyone" (Romans 12:18; see also Hebrews 12:14). That's right, everyone—including Muslims.

Thomas Davis had lived in Padang on the island of Sumatra in Indonesia, a number of years ago. Because of this, he was invited to speak at the Muhammadiyah University there recently. He began his speech with an apology. "I have come from America to ask for forgiveness because we American Christians have not loved our Muslim neighbors in America as Jesus commanded us to." The surprised crowd sat eagerly waiting to hear more. So Thomas shared Jesus' teaching on love and reconciliation, highlighting where followers of Jesus in America have fallen short.

He then continued with some good news. "There is a growing number of Christians in America, like those of us in Peace Catalyst International, who want to live according to the teachings of Jesus." He explained how he does this by giving practical examples of his own peacemaking work with Muslims in the city of Raleigh.

When Thomas finished speaking, a Muslim professor from another university stood up and gave an impassioned challenge: "Thomas has come from America to bring a message from God. He and his co-workers are modeling for Indonesian Muslims a better way to live. Indonesian Muslims must learn to treat Indonesian Christians with kindness and respect. We need to follow Thomas' example of serving the minority, learning from them and building friendships with them."

Thomas was just trying to be faithful and tell his story. He worked for peace within his sphere of influence. The result? His story planted seeds for peace and greater religious freedom in Indonesia.

2. Christians need to partner with Muslims to counter terrorism and promote religious freedom.

Douglas Johnston and his organization, the International Center for Faith and Diplomacy (www.icrd.org), partners with Muslims to promote religious freedom and counter terrorism in Pakistan.[1]

For the past ten years they have worked with Muslim leaders of *madrasas* (religious schools) to expand their curriculum beyond the Qur'an. They have engaged over 1,611 *madrasas*, enlarging their curriculum to include sciences, along with a strong emphasis on religious tolerance and human rights.

Johnston wisely notes, "Bombs typically create additional terrorists by exacerbating the cycle of revenge. Education, on the other hand, both drains the swamp of extremism and provides a better future for the children of Pakistan (and, indirectly, for our own as well)."[2]

Think about this: Christians and Muslims comprise over half the world's population. If we can't have peace between them, then it will be virtually impossible to have peace in the world.

The Bible says, "seek peace and pursue it" (1 Peter 3:11). I would add: in your own sphere of influence and in partnership with Muslim peacemakers. These two keys will unleash peace!

So pray that Christians will emulate the Prince of Peace. Pray that God will raise up thousands of Muslim peacemakers with whom we can partner.

Check out Recommended Resources on page 28 ▼

To learn more about peacemaking, see Rick's book, Peace Catalysts: Resolving Conflict in Our Families, Organizations and Communities. *Or visit www.peace-catalyst.net*

[1] http://peace-catalyst.net/blog/post/peacemaking-in-pakistan:-promoting-religious-freedom
[2] David Gushee (ed). *Evangelical Peacemakers*, (2013), p57. http://amzn.to/Ufl1HL

The Uzbek speakers of Southern Kyrgyzstan

There are approximately 800,000 Uzbek speakers in southern Kyrgyzstan, including Uyghurs and Turks, as well as ethnic Uzbeks. Most of these people live near to the border with Uzbekistan, in the Kyrgyzstan part of the Fergana Valley. This agriculturally rich region is one of the most densely populated areas in Central Asia. Competition for trade, land and water has often been a point of conflict, particularly between different ethnic groups.

Over the last decade, there has been a rise in Kyrgyz nationalism that has made life difficult for the Uzbek-speaking minorities. This pressure has intensified since inter-ethnic rioting in 2010, with discrimination in legal and political spheres and loss of economic opportunities. Nearly all Uzbek speakers identify themselves as Muslims, but recently the influence of Islam has grown, accompanied by an increase in fundamentalism.

Outwardly, more people are finding their identity in Islam, but some are genuinely seeking God. Nadim is an Uzbek speaker who lives in rural Kyrgyzstan with his wife and five children. He had been suffering with recurring nightmares for over 20 years, seeking treatment from many doctors and psychologists. Nadim knew that it would take a miracle for his nightmares to stop, and was considering a trip to Mecca when he met withbelievers who were able to pray with him and his family. The bad dreams continued on and off but every time someone prayed for him in Jesus' name he had a peaceful night's sleep. He is now free from these nightmares altogether. Since receiving a New Testament, Nadim carries it around in his pocket. Through his eagerness to study scripture, his whole family and their networks also have the opportunity to hear God's Word.

HOW CAN WE PRAY?

- *Pray for seekers like Nadim, that they would encounter Jesus through believers, through signs and wonders, and through God's Word.*
- *Pray that not only individuals, but also families and whole networks would come into the kingdom.*
- *Pray for justice and hope for Uzbek-speaking minorities in southern Kyrgyzstan.*

Turkestan: The living Christ

Turkestan is the land of 200 million Turkic peoples comprising 227 Turkic people groups in 15 nations. It stretches 4,000 miles across the steppes of Central Asia, from its place of ethnic origins in the Altai Mountains on Mongolia's western border through the turbulent Caucasus region before spilling into modern-day Turkey and the Balkan states of Europe.

Since the Ottoman conquest of Constantinople in 1453, Muslim Turks have laid claim to Turkestan as an Islamic stronghold. Over the past two decades, however, God's Spirit has been stirring in Turkestan, drawing thousands of Central Asian Turks to new life in Jesus Christ.

This awakening began in the 1940s, when Josef Stalin relocated thousands of ethnic German evangelicals to Central Asia. Fearing their presence near the frontlines of the war with Germany, he intended to exile them to the Turkestani hinterlands. Unwittingly, he positioned them in the middle of one of the greatest concentrations of Muslims on earth.

After the collapse of the Iron Curtain in 1989, thousands of Western evangelical missionaries entered Central Asia for the first time, bringing with them Bible translations, Christian gospel media, and ministries that conveyed the love and compassion of Jesus Christ.

Today, many churches have been shut and Western ministries expelled, but Turkestani Muslim-background believers are nevertheless gathering in underground fellowships and quietly sharing the love and power of the gospel with their friends and families.

When asked what God used to bring them to faith in Jesus Christ, Turkestani Muslim-background believers described the role of dreams, the importance of having a New Testament in their own language, watching the *Jesus* film, and other factors. But the most important thread linking each testimony was the discovery of a living Christ who heard and answered their prayers. Unlike the empty offerings of communism, cultural Islam, or secular atheism, the living Christ had touched a deep place in their soul that nothing else had ever filled.

HOW CAN WE PRAY?

- *Pray for the persecuted Muslim-background believers and churches of Turkestan.*
- *Pray that the current oppression of Christian missions to Turkestan would lead local Turkestani Muslim-background believers to evangelize more boldly.*
- *Pray for the thousands of Turkestani villages that have no gospel witness whatsoever.*

TURKESTAN	
Nations	15
Muslim people groups	227
Total population	203,251,345
Muslim population	159,225,454

Russia
Kazakhstan
Bosnia & Herzegovina
Serbia
Bulgaria Armenia Uzbekistan Kyrgyzstan China
Kosovo Turkey Turkmenistan
Montenegro Azerbaijan
Iraq Afghanistan

Bosnia-Herzegovina: Culture, conflict and the cross

The beautiful country of Bosnia-Herzegovina was the setting for one of the most devastating wars of the late 20th century. If you walk down the streets of Sarajevo today, bullet-hole-ridden walls are reminders that it endured a tortuous siege lasting nearly four years. One of the deadliest episodes in this war was the execution of 8,000 Bosnian Muslim men and boys in the town of Srebrenica by Bosnian Serb forces. Religious nationalism in Bosnia-Herzegovina became an idol that brought savage destruction. Ethnic wars make sharing Jesus so much more challenging.

The roots of this conflict extend back to 1389, when a Turkish Muslim army was victorious over the ethnic Serbians. In the 1990s, as communism fell these old ethnic rivalries re-emerged; fighting broke out again between Serbians (who were Orthodox Christians), Croatians (Catholics) and Bosnian Muslims. Religion was used by all sides, and the cross of Jesus, the ultimate symbol of love, was raised as a standard by both Catholic Croat forces and Orthodox Serb forces.

The war was immensely complicated, and many atrocities were committed on all sides. The war was not a religious one, yet religion brought definition to the different ethnic groups. Christianity was used as justification for war and a motivation to fight. How far this was from the Jesus who told a people under brutal Roman occupation to "love your enemies." How far this religious tribalism was from the Jesus who said it didn't matter what mountain we worshiped Him on, but what was important was that we would worship the Father in Spirit and truth (John 4:21–24).

How can we expect Muslims in Bosnia-Herzegovina today to convert to the religion of those who committed the Srebrenica massacre? How can they understand the truth of what Jesus did on the cross when it has been so tainted by the war? Yet the Muslims of Bosnia-Herzegovina desperately need to meet Jesus, the Prince of Peace.

HOW CAN WE PRAY?

- *That followers of Jesus in Bosnia-Herzegovina will be courageous witnesses to the beauty of the grace-soaked gospel of Jesus.*
- *That young Bosnian Muslims will be protected from the excesses of extremism and develop a hunger only Jesus can fill. Pray they will have dreams of Jesus.*
- *For a deep reconciliation to permeate this land, leading to a turning to Jesus, the one in whom there is no Jew or Greek, Croatian, Serb, Bosnian, Muslim, Orthodox or Catholic.*

Western South Asia: Change is coming

Comprising the nations of Afghanistan and Pakistan and the western half of India, Western South Asia spans the fault lines of competing Hindu, Turkic, Persian, and Dravidian civilizations that have spawned generations of conflict among the region's 315 million Muslims in 186 distinct people groups.

Unlike some corners of the Muslim world, where wives and daughters are subjected to *purdah* (the practice of hiding women from public as a tribute to their great value), tribal Muslims from the remote interior of Western South Asia harbor no such illusions. They value women only as property.

A Muslim-background believer named Ahmed explains, "In our culture, women are like shoes. We wear them, and when they are old we throw them out. If a woman does something that does not please her husband, he will drag her through the streets to the cemetery and bury her alive."

For the believers in Western South Asia, this behavior is changing. A turning point occurred when two female American missionaries arranged a workshop for a dozen women from tribal Muslim villages. At the last minute, the women's husbands came instead!

Donna, one of the teachers, recalls, "The first day was a fiasco. The tribal men were aghast at the thought of two women teaching them anything." During an awkward conversation with the American women, Ahmed casually asked, "Should we not be beating our wives. What does the Bible say?" An earnest discussion followed, with Donna pointing out many relevant scriptures about how men should treat their wives with sacrificial love.

The next morning Ahmed said, "All night we did not sleep. We talked about what Jesus says about women, and how we should treat our wives." One by one the men stood and said, "I will no longer beat my wife. After today, we will treat our wives with respect."

Could it be that simple? "It's not been easy," Ahmed admitted. "That was a big change for us."

After the workshop a women's movement was launched, which has started hundreds of women's *jamaats* (churches). The men requested more training for reaching the women. "Last year," Ahmed said, "more than 100 *jamaat* leaders said to me, 'I no longer beat my wife.'"

HOW CAN WE PRAY?

- *Pray for an end to war, conflict, killing, and injustice in Western South Asia.*
- *Pray for the continued growth in Christ-likeness of the new believers in Western South Asia.*
- *Pray that God would continue to give birth to new movements of Muslims to faith and new life in Jesus Christ.*

WESTERN SOUTH ASIA WORLD	
Nations	3
Muslim people groups	186
Total population	713,922,175
Muslim population	315,998,874

Marathi-speaking Shaikhs

> They have a deep sense of devotion to Allah.

There are over 200 million Shaikh Muslims in the world; most live in India, Pakistan and Bangladesh. Shaikh Muslims form the majority of the Sunni Muslim population in the Deccan plateau of Central India. Marathi-speaking Shaikh Muslims are rural people, living primarily in the state of Maharashtra where Marathi is the state language. The total estimated population of Marathi-speaking Shaikh is 2.5 million.

The term "Shaikh" once applied only to tribes of pure Arab descent, but now covers specific Islamic peoples in central and southern India who converted from low Hindu castes three or more generations ago and for those who converted from high Hindu castes in north India through the work of Islamic Sufi missionaries. Sometimes Indian Shaikh communities are distinct from the other Muslims, but more often they intermix.

The Shaikh do not have traditional occupations. In rural areas they are generally employed as agricultural laborers. In urban areas they are relatively well educated and so are employed in trade and in government and private service sectors.

Virtually all Shaikh are Sunni Muslims, though their practices may be unorthodox. As a whole, Islam in India includes strong elements of mysticism. Veneration of local Muslim saints is common, and their graves are extravagantly decorated and worship and playing devotional music take place there. They have a deep sense of devotion to Allah. Sufi teachings have led many Shaikh to believe in universalism — that all religious paths ultimately lead to Allah.

The Marathi-speaking Shaikh celebrate major Sunni Muslim festivals and holy days. Children receive basic religious education, and in recent years the ever-growing Indian middle classes are able to ensure their children continue to higher education. With recent economic development, some have been deeply influenced by secularism and materialism.

There is no Bible or related literature in the Shaikh version of the Marathi language, though a traditional Marathi-language Bible is widely available. Many also speak Urdu or Hindi, and Bibles and the *Jesus* film are available in those languages.

HOW CAN WE PRAY?

- *Pray that the Marathi-speaking Shaikh farmers who hear the gospel would understand and respond in faith.*
- *Pray for recent believers from among the Marathi-speaking Shaikh, that they would become grounded in the Word, daily growing in faith, love, and obedience to God.*
- *Pray for creative ways to reach the Marathi-speaking Shaikh who are illiterate. Pray that God would provide the tools (audio Scriptures, stories, etc.) as well as avenues for mass distribution.*

Eastern South Asia: A Bible of our own

Eastern South Asia is a crowded Room of more than 800 million inhabitants, of whom nearly 250 million are Muslims. The Room centers around the Bengali people of Bangladesh and India's state of West Bengal, but also encompasses 64 other Muslim people groups. In the midst, the Holy Spirit is giving new life in Jesus Christ to multiple movements of Muslims.

When missionary William Carey published the first Bengali Bible in 1809, most Bengalis were either Hindus or Muslims. Carey knew his choice of religious vocabulary would incline the Bible toward either the Muslim or Hindu population. Carey tilted toward the Hindu, choosing the Sanskrit-based word *Ishwar* to translate the word 'God' rather than *Allah* or *Khoda*, words

EASTERN SOUTH ASIA	
Nations	4
Muslim people groups	65
Total population	844,398,260
Muslim population	283,393,591

used by Muslims.

For the next 170 years, Carey's choice convinced Muslims that Christians worshiped some other god, likely one from the Hindu pantheon. In the early 1970s, when translators produced the first gospel portions of the contextualized Muslim translation they adopted the word *Khoda* for God — an Urdu-language loan word commonly used by both Muslims and Christians in East and West Pakistan.

After the 1971 War of Liberation with West Pakistan, Bangladeshis distanced themselves from Urdu and began using the name Allah for God. Seeking to communicate with Muslims, when translators published the complete *Musulmani* (synonym for Muslim) *Bengali Common Language Bible* in the year 2000, they chose the word *Allah* for God. Though Christians in the West associate the name Allah with Islam, it is, in fact, Christian in origin. The translators knew that what distinguishes Christians from Muslims is not the name they use for God, but their

theological understanding of God, and that the only way to correct the Muslim understanding of God was to give them the complete Bible in their own language.

With the appearance of the *Musulmani Bengali Bible*, many Muslims in Eastern South Asia are reading the Bible for themselves and coming to understand that the God of the Bible is not a Hindu deity, but the One who loves them enough to offer His own Son as a sacrifice and Savior from their sins.

HOW CAN WE PRAY?

- *Pray that many Muslims in Eastern South Asia would meet the God of the Bible through new local translations.*
- *Pray for love and harmony between Christians from non-Muslim and Muslim backgrounds.*
- *Pray for the millions of Muslims in Eastern South Asia who have never heard the gospel of Jesus Christ.*

Recommended Resources

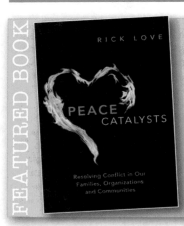

RICK LOVE

PEACE CATALYSTS

Resolving Conflict in Our Families, Organizations and Communities

Peace Catalysts
Rick Love

Conflict happens. It's a painful reality of life in a fallen world. But we don't need to be content with broken relationships. God's intention for us and for the world is for all to live in peace with one another, and Christian peacemakers have an unparalleled opportunity to be ambassadors of reconciliation. With the life of Jesus as the prime example, Love seeks to empower peacemakers of all stripes to integrate evangelical witness with commitment to reconciliation. We can walk in the footsteps of Jesus as catalysts of peace, bringing transformation and hope to a world crying out for healing and forgiveness—in the home and workplace and even across inter religious and international borders. *$15.00 Sale Price: $12.00*

American Christians often opt for an ethic that has more in common with the story of Muhammad than with the story of Jesus. This book shows readers how to be faithful to Jesus while figuring out how to respond to Muslims in today's world, as well as to the New Atheists who suppose that all religion is inherently violent. *$18.00 Sale Price: $14.40*

A Muslim's Mind
Edward Hoskins
Most Christian workers rely on the Qur'an as their primary source for understanding Muslims. But it is actually the so-called Islamic traditions (the *Hadiths*) that influence Muslim thought and behavior more than anything else. The author (a physician and Navigator missionary with a heart for the Muslim

In the House of Islam DVD
ISIS! Boko Haram! These radical terror groups invade our news channels every day. But there is an even greater story unfolding across the Muslim world today. The author of the acclaimed book *A Wind in the House of Islam* Dr David Garrison traveled more than a quarter-million miles into every corner of the House of Islam to investigate unprecedented reports of multiplying movements of Muslims who were turning to faith in Jesus Christ. On this video you will learn about what Muslims believe, their practices, their heart desires, and how they are responding as never before to the gospel of Jesus Christ. (56-, 31- and 17-minute versions on same DVD.) *$22.99 Sale Price: $16.09*

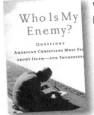

Who Is My Enemy?
Lee Camp
Camp shatters misconceptions about religious violence, arguing that

community) has spent years going through approximately 35,000 respected Arab Islamic traditions, condensing and organizing them into helpful topics.

$12.99 ***Sale Price: $11.04***

2016 Personal Prayer Diary/ Planner

YWAM (ships in October)
36th annual edition. For over 30 years believers have used this tool to organize their daily, weekly and monthly schedules, journal their prayer times and Bible reading, and systematically pray for the nations of the world. These Diaries are a proven classic! They are more than practical planners; they are a devotional and global experience! Closed-loop spiral-bound in green, blue, burgundy or black, 7x9 inches.

$17.99 ***Sale Price: $12.59***

You've Got Libya

Greg Livingstone
This is Greg Livingstone's autobiography —
"An utterly real, high-impact, sham-free life story." (Don Richardson). Greg spent a lifetime planting churches in Muslim communities, and can testify to the life-changing power of the gospel. The narrative is full of compelling humor and self-deprecating honesty. The result is a page-turning *tour de force* that urges the reader to pursue God unreservedly and to join with Him in the adventure of pursuing the lost. Greg launched "Frontiers", a mission agency that has grown to a movement of more than one thousand field workers among Muslim communities.

$16.99 ***Sale Price: $13.59***

Connecting With Muslims

Fouad Masri
How can we build bridges with Muslims, who may have become neighbors, coworkers or friends? You don't need a PhD in Islam to share your faith with a Muslim, you just need the heart of an ambassador. Masri provides practical ways for Christians to initiate conversations, and offers insights that help Christians to understand and relate to their Muslim friends. He addresses seven common questions that Muslims ask about the Christian faith, providing sensitive answers that guide Muslims to Jesus without arguing or awkward debating. With real-life stories of fruitful conversations and genuine relationships, he helps readers see Muslims as Jesus sees them.

$15.00 ***Sale Price: $12.75***

Just for Kids

The family/ children's edition of the prayer booklet you are holding in your hand. It follows the same daily prayer topics (shortened and simplified for elementary school-age kids), and also includes some fun activities. Involve the younger members of your church and family!

$3.50 (discounts start at 10 copies)

Order these resources online at www.WorldChristian.com or see the order form on page 56.

Kanpur: 'Manchester of the East'

Located on the banks of the Ganges River, Kanpur is one of north India's major industrial and educational centers. With a population around four million, Kanpur is the largest city in the state of Uttar Pradesh. Hinduism is the most prominent religion, but around 20 percent of the population is Muslim, most of whom are poor and illiterate. Communal violence and riots are common, and many Muslims seem to have nothing to lose except their lives.

Kanpur has a long history of violence. It has been the scene of some of India's most memorable struggles for freedom and clashes between people of different politics, cultures and religions. The First War of Independence, also called the Indian Sepoy Mutiny of 1857, was the first widespread uprising against the British East India Company. Around 300 British were killed at a place now called

It has been the scene of some of India's most memorable struggles for freedom.

Massacre Ghat, followed by another massacre at Bibighar, where around 120 British women and children were dismembered and thrown into a dry well — in reaction, some historians believe, to news of violence by the East India Company rescue force coming from Allahabad.

Communal riots and criminal gangs have stained Kanpur's past. The famous Kanpur Mosque incident in 1913 became the first symbol of Indian national Muslim politics. The British wanted to demolish/move the mosque washing facilities to construct a road. This was seen as a threat to Islam, so committees were formed and riots followed.

In 1931, independence movement activist Ganesh Shankar Vidyarthi (founder and editor of the revolutionary Hindi newspaper, *Pratap*, and leader of the Indian National Congress) died in Muslim–Hindu riots that killed an

estimated 166 and injured 480. In 1992, Kala Bacha ("black child"), a known criminal allied to the BJP political party, was active in riots in Kanpur, including those following the demolition of Babri Masjid mosque in Ayodhya (200km from Kanpur). In 2001, the demolition of the Buddha statues of Bamiyan in Afghanistan and the subsequent burning of the Qu'ran in Delhi by Hindus also triggered riots in Kanpur involving members of the Students Islamic Movement of India.

HOW CAN WE PRAY?

- *God wants to restore peace to Kanpur. Pray for reconciliation between religious groups.*
- *Pray that God's love and compassion would be displayed through the few Christians who live in Kanpur and that His Body will be revived and filled with the love of God.*
- *Pray that God would send more workers to Kanpur to bring the message of the Prince of Peace.*

Indo-Malaysia: Three waves

INDO-MALAYSIA	
Nations	6
Muslim people groups	282
Total population	283,696,115
Muslim population	201,000,020

The Indo-Malaysia Room in the House of Islam extends from the Malay Peninsula through the Indonesian archipelago and into the surrounding nations of Singapore, Brunei, the Philippines, and southern Thailand. It is home to more than 200 million Muslims. Today's multiple movements of Muslims to Christ began in 1870 with the ministry of one Muslim-background believer in Indonesia called Sadrach Surapranata.

By 1873, Sadrach had seen more than 2,500 Javanese Muslims turn from Islam to faith in Jesus Christ, something no Christian had witnessed in the 1,238 years since the death of the Prophet Muhammad. By the time of his death in 1924, the number of Indonesian Muslim-background believers was estimated at 10–20,000 baptized Christians.

Muslim movements to Christ in this region fall into three distinct waves. The first was Sadrach's pioneering breakthrough. The second occurred from 1967–1971, when an attempted communist coup led to the violent suppression of communism, and all Indonesians were required to declare allegiance to one of the nation's five accepted religions — Islam, Hinduism, Buddhism, Catholicism or Protestantism. Some half a million Indonesians were killed by vigilante Islamic forces, leading some 2.8 million Indonesians to join the Protestant faith, perhaps the largest turning of Muslims to Christ in history.

The third wave is happening right now. The growth of the Church in Indonesia today continues in a less dramatic, but equally pervasive manner. In the Indo-Malaysia Room, more and more Muslims are hearing the gospel of Jesus Christ today through their native tongues and responding to the love of Jesus Christ. Breakthroughs are occurring through innovations in the presentation of the gospel, bold contextualized gospel witness, and the faithful witness of local Christians that now extends into every corner of this crowded Room in the House of Islam.

HOW CAN WE PRAY?

- Pray that the gospel will continue to reach into every corner in the Indo-Malaysian Room.
- Pray for Muslims coming to faith in Christ as they endure persecution and make a bold stand for Jesus Christ.
- Pray for Christians and missionaries whose courage and innovation continue to reach out to the region's 282 Muslim people groups.

Pattani Malays of Thailand

The Pattani Malay people group is an ethnic community of devout Muslim people of Malay descent living in southern Thailand. They number about 3.5 million.

The Pattani Malay have a rich cultural heritage and are highly skilled craftsmen. These skills can be seen in their colorful fishing boats called *korlae* and other handicrafts. Many earn their living by fishing, working in fish factories, tapping rubber, or farming vegetables or fruits. Generally, however, Muslims in southern Thailand earn less than the minimum wage. Many are caught in a poverty cycle exacerbated by low income and high birth rates.

The provinces where most Pattani Malay live are a long way from the center of Thai government, and the Pattani Malay have developed a sense of uniqueness and independence. However, each time the government tries to centralize control in their provinces, this independence is threatened, resulting in resentment toward the government.

Most Pattani Malay speak a dialect of Malay. Thai is rarely spoken in the village context, though it is used at school and when dealing with government officials or Thai Buddhists. Pattani Malay remains their heart language.

The Pattani Malay generally live in close-knit communities, and social acceptance is important. Young people are increasingly influenced by TV and films though, and drug addiction and immorality are on the rise. Economic and political problems are found alongside environmental ones; this often undermines the Pattani Malay's traditional way of life. Pattani Malays live in a time of crisis, with violent responses to instability becoming a growing concern.

Unlike most of the population of Thailand, who are Buddhist, the Pattani Malay are Muslim. Throughout all the recent changes and crises the Pattani Malays have experienced, Islam has been a constant. Since the beginnings of the ancient Malay kingdom in Thailand, Islam has had a major influence on their culture. They closely adhere to Islamic law, or *sharia*, which is taught in the traditional Islamic schools called *pondoks*. Due to their dedication to the Islamic faith, the Pattani Malay have a distinct identity in Thailand.

HOW CAN WE PRAY?

- *For affordable educational opportunities to be developed that will help break the cycle of poverty for the Pattani Malay.*
- *That more Pattani Malay will read and hear the story of Jesus and experience His transforming power.*
- *Ask the Holy Spirit to grant wisdom and favor to missions agencies and workers focusing on this people group.*

Bridges of God in the Muslim World (part one)

A survey of more than a thousand Muslim-background believers from movements to Christ throughout the House of Islam asked the question: "What did God use to bring you to faith in Jesus Christ?" Their answers revealed ten insights into the bridges of God — the ways He is drawing Muslims to Christ. Here are the first five:

(1) Faith

By faith, earlier generations of Christian missionaries entered the House of Islam to proclaim a gospel that was met with stiff resistance. Many of these missionaries never saw the movements that are occurring today — "they only saw them and welcomed them from a distance" (Hebrews 11:13). Their faith helped to produce today's unprecedented harvest (Hebrews 12:1).

(2) Prayer

In the last 14 centuries, there have only been 82 documented Muslim movements to Christ. Of these, 69 have taken place over the past two decades.

It's no accident that these contemporary Muslim movements to Christ coincide with the fervent prayer accompanying the *30 Days of Prayer for the Muslim World*. Your prayers are effectively opening the door (Revelation 3:8) for Muslims to hear and respond to the gospel as never before.

(3) Scripture

God promised that His word would not return to Him empty (Isaiah 55:11), but unless the Bible is translated into the languages of the lost how can it be understood and believed (Romans 10:14)? More Scripture has been translated into the heart languages of Muslims over the past three decades than in the preceding 13 centuries.

(4) Holy Spirit activity

Jesus promised that the Holy Spirit would "convict the world of guilt in regard to sin and righteousness and judgment" (John 16:8). Ahead of every Muslim movement to Christ throughout the House of Islam, the Holy Spirit has been convicting through dreams, visions, divine encounters, and answered prayers.

(5) Faithful Christian witness

Today's Muslim movements to Christ are the result of countless faithful Christians from every branch of the Church who have ever shared the gospel with Muslims.

HOW CAN WE PRAY?

- Pray for an increase in Faith, Prayer, Scripture, Holy Spirit activity, and Faithful Christian witness to the Muslim world.
- Pray that Christians will cross these five bridges that God has provided to take the good news to the House of Islam.
- Ask God to show you what He would have you do personally to cross these bridges.

Syrian refugees: Not that different to me

Yusra is a 39-year-old Syrian Muslim woman. Hers, like most refugee homes, was a three-generation home. Her seven children were sprinkled around the room, and her incredibly wrinkly mother was perched on a cushion on the floor. At one point, the old woman began to rant about the horrors she'd seen and the pain that racked her body and soul. I scooted off my mat, grabbed her hand, and offered to pray for her in the name of Jesus, the One who heals. Her rant turned into a groan, and tears streamed down her face as she told us about her missing sons.

We then visited the family downstairs. Jake chatted with the men about politics and war while the women talked about family, loss and pain. As we stood to leave, the grandmother, Umm Ahmad, kissed me, placed her hands on my womb, and cried out, "May God bless you with twins! May he give you double abundance because your heart is pure and you prayed for our family!" I had recently miscarried. Her words struck my heart as if a loving arrow was released straight from the heart of God.

When I told her that we had recently lost our child, she grabbed my hand and held it for a long time. For a moment, she climbed out of her ocean of pain and into our little world to comfort us. Then she pointed at her daughter-in-law and whispered, "She lost one the same day as you. May God return to you what was taken."

Yusra then came downstairs for a visit. Umm Ahmad began blessing me again: "May God give you two sets of twins!" I smiled, and looked at Yusra, who had twins. She told us that she'd actually had two sets of twins, but she'd miscarried one set last year. We allowed the silence to hover as we sipped our hot tea and shared a small cup of each other's pain.

Yusra broke the sorrowful silence, shouting out something funny. We laughed; at that moment all of us — people normally separated by boundaries, countries and cultures — felt the same.

HOW CAN WE PRAY?

- Pray that believers would be a loving testimony as they open their arms to the refugees.
- Pray for Syrian refugees to be empowered with hope and practical help to stand and rebuild their lives.
- Pray for rapidly multiplying church-planting movements to break out and spread among Syrian refugees.

Bridges of God in the Muslim World (part two)

Our survey of more than a thousand Muslim-background believers revealed multiple bridges that God is using today. The first five (see page 33) came as no surprise. The next five were less predictable.

(6) Learning from the Body of Christ

Today, Christ's disciples are learning from the emerging Body of Christ within the House of Islam about how to reach Muslims. Breakthroughs in Indonesia lead to new movements in sub-Saharan Africa; new approaches from South Asia are producing new fruit in Central Asia. To reach the Muslim world for Christ we must be humble learners.

> Our challenge is to create means by which Muslims can discover for themselves the good news of Jesus Christ.

(7) Communication

The gospel is being proclaimed more widely and effectively than ever before. Technological advances are spreading the gospel message in ways unimaginable only a few decades ago. Christians are using contextualized gospel translations and methods of witness that are allowing Muslims to hear the message of the gospel without being distracted by the cultural trappings of those proclaiming it.

(8) Discovery

Historically, Muslims have resisted being told they are lost and in need of the gospel, but when they discover it for themselves — through encounters with the living Christ — they are gripped by the same power of the gospel message that captivates believers everywhere. Our challenge is to create means by which Muslims can discover for themselves the good news of Jesus Christ.

(9) Islam itself

This is a surprise to many Christians, yet many Muslim-background believers report that reading the Qur'an in their own language, rather than in Arabic, is how God first revealed to them that they were lost and in need of a Savior.

(10) Indigenization

"Indigenization" means "generated from within." Though Muslim movements to Christ begin when someone from outside their world brings them the good news, it takes root and multiplies when it is "owned" by the Muslim-background believers and translated into their own culture and worldview.

HOW CAN WE PRAY?

- *Pray that Christians will recognize the importance of these five bridges and cross them to take the good news to the House of Islam.*
- *Pray that these bridges would draw more Muslims to faith in Christ.*
- *Ask God how He would have you cross these bridges to bring the good news of Jesus Christ to Muslims in your own community.*

The Night of Power: Expecting God!

Muslims recognize many historic events that are significant in the story of their faith. None are more important, however, than remembering the initial revelation of the Qur'an to the Prophet Muhammad. This is the event recalled on the Night of Power, or *Laylat Al-Qadr* — also known as the Night of Destiny.

The story of Muhammad's revelation is told to Muslim children throughout the world and is an inspiration for them.

It is said that Muhammad would frequently retire to meditate in a cave on the outskirts of Mecca. He would reflect on how to solve the problems faced in the communities around him, particularly among the less fortunate, and how to address the rise in selfish and abusive behavior in society.

In the month of Ramadan in AD 610, Muhammad was visited by the Archangel Gabriel. According to sources, Gabriel squeezed the Prophet to the point of death and commanded him, *Iqraa* — Read! Muhammad was illiterate and responded that he couldn't. This was repeated two times. Then Gabriel revealed the first verses of the Qur'an:

"Read in the name of your Lord who created — created man from a clot. Read: for your Lord is Most Bountiful, who teaches by the pen, teaches man that which he knew not." (Chapter 96, verses 1–5)

> **Many Muslims believe that prayers prayed on the Night of Power are more effective**

When Muhammad told a relative, who was a biblical scholar, about this, the relative advised him that he had been chosen as a prophet and was sent by God to call society to worship the One God and lead a righteous life.

To remember this event, Muslims spend the last ten days of Ramadan in increased worship, recitation of the Qur'an and fervent prayer, particularly for the forgiveness of sins. The Night of Power is understood to have occurred in this time, probably on this night (the 26th). Many Muslims believe that prayers prayed on the Night of Power are more effective and will be counted as a thousand times more beneficial.

It is a night for anticipating the revelation of God. Let's pray that it happens.

HOW CAN WE PRAY?

● *Many Muslims have had dreams or visions of Jesus on the Night of Power. Pray that through Jesus many will come to have the revelation of God that they desire.*

● *Pray for Muslims who are seeking revelation to have encounters with believers who can help them to understand the revelation we have of God through Jesus.*

● *Pray that on this night of heightened expectation, many will find what they are seeking.*

Faith for the miraculous

Syrian refugees have flooded the safe borders of Jordan, and are filling our neighborhoods. The church I attend with local Arab Christians is embracing, loving and helping these precious people who have lost so much. Groups of Syrians now beg to be prayed for in the name of Jesus! They're experiencing His power to answer prayer, and growing in openness to Him.

Not long ago I met Umm Bader, a Muslim Syrian lady who sits in the second row in church every Sunday, head covered, unashamed of how she is different from the Christians sitting around her. She is an older widow, bowed over with a crooked back and gnarled hands, perhaps from all the hardships she's endured. Some of her children are dead; some are still in Syria, recently found because Jesus answered her prayers to locate them. The following is a miraculous story she shared:

Recently, someone named Isa came to her house at 2:30am and gave her 100 Jordanian dinar (about US$141). She thought it was a man called Isa from church, but when that man said he had most certainly been at home sleeping next to his wife at that hour, she realized it must have been Isa *Al-Maseeh*. Jesus the Messiah!

That same morning she requested prayer at church because her grandson had been taken by the extremist group ISIS and was scheduled to be tried by them — a fate that meant certain death. She discovered later that at the very same hour Jesus visited her in the night, her grandson was released by ISIS. The extremist judging him gave no reason; he simply looked at him and told him to leave. Those who were tried before him were slaughtered. Her grandson arrived home the same day. Impossible. It was a miraculous outcome!

Often, Umm Bader stands up boldly in a church full of Arab Christians, modestly dressed in Muslim garb, and glorifies Jesus for answering her prayers. Our Arab pastor keeps exhorting the flock, saying we should all have faith like Umm Bader.

HOW CAN WE PRAY?

- *That Jesus will appear to many Syrian refugees and show them His love and Lordship.*
- *That believers in Jesus all over the world will open their arms to love the refugees and open their mouths to share the good news with them.*
- *For rapidly multiplying church-planting movements to break out and spread among Syrian refugees.*

Barriers to movements

During this past 150 years, we have seen 82 Muslim movements to Christ; whether or not this pattern will continue remains to be seen. Some of the greatest barriers facing Muslims coming to Christ are within the community of Christ itself. Five barriers that must be removed for the gospel to spread effectively throughout the House of Islam are:

(1) Contentious Christians
With more than 40,000 denominations today, Christianity is irreparably fragmented, but that doesn't mean we need to fight one another. We must turn our focus on the gospel and not on our differences.

(2) Fear and hatred
When Christians feel threatened by Muslims, our fear can turn to anger and hatred. The threat of Islam is not hollow: Islam is a totalitarian ideology that crushes dissent wherever it arises. But Muslims are not an ideology; they are men and women lost without a Savior. Christ alone offers the "perfect love (that) casts out fear" (1 John 4:18) that can empower us to win the Muslim world to Him.

(3) Imitating Islam
Islam elevated a seventh-century culture as God's ideal for the world, exalted its scripture to the status of deity, imposed a legalistic path to heaven, threatened apostates and critics with death, and advanced its boundaries with military might. At one time or another, Christians have attempted the same. But these aren't the ways of Jesus nor the path that He prescribes for His followers. Winning the Muslim world to Christ will only occur through the way of Christ and not through a misguided imitation of Islam.

(4) Ignored injustice
As Arab armies advanced into the Christian Byzantine world, they found a civilization that had embraced the Christian religion yet ignored many injustices, such as slavery. Islamic jurists declared that no Christian master could own a Muslim slave, leading to the immediate conversion of thousands of slaves to Islam. When Christians ignore societal injustices, we open the door to Islam.

(5) Ignorance and apathy
For more than five centuries, Christians in the West could ignore the challenge of Islam. That changed on September 11 2001, when Western ignorance and apathy crashed to the ground with the World Trade Towers. To participate in God's great global ingathering of Muslims, we must shake off ignorance and apathy in engaging with the Muslim world.

HOW CAN WE PRAY?

● *Pray that Christians around the world will address each of these barriers and take action to change them into bridges that will introduce Christ to the Muslim world.*

> Some of the greatest barriers facing Muslims coming to Christ are within the community of Christ itself.

The Nanumba of Ghana

Abdallah is one of around 100,000 people who identify as Nanumbas. With his family, he lives in the traditional capital of his people group — Bimbilla, which is located in the southeastern corner of the northern region of Ghana. As a true Nanumba, Abdallah was brought up a Muslim. However, in his daily life animism plays an equally significant role.

Asked why he became a Christian, he tells this story with a smile, "Because I have seen the light! I had been seeing it now and then for many years, an indescribably pure light. It was different from the lights I had seen in connection with witchcraft or evil spirits! One night in my dream I saw this light rising over my daughter. Shortly after that, a pastor from a brother tribe came to my house and invited my daughter to get schooling at his wife's school. Because of the dream, I agreed. I even allowed her to tell us what she had learned during school devotions."

"At that time I was seriously ill. One day, the headmistress felt led to pray for the sick relatives of her pupils. That morning while lying on my mat I suddenly saw the light and was instantly healed. When my daughter told me about the prayers, I knew where the healing had come from, and started attending church with her. The pastor took time to explain the gospel to me and after some weeks my daughter and I trusted Jesus as our Lord and Savior."

In this remote corner of a remote region of western Africa, the light of Jesus is shining like a candle in the darkness.

HOW CAN WE PRAY?

- *That God prepares many other Nanumbas for an encounter with Christians.*
- *That the few Christians in Bimbilla (mainly workers from other tribes) develop a zeal to reach out to the Nanumbas.*
- *For new converts like Abdallah, that they grow in faith and become bold witnesses.*

Practical steps

God is at work in the Muslim world today. His Spirit is drawing countless thousands of Muslims to new life in Jesus. But how can we participate in what God is doing? Here are five steps we can take right now:

(1) Pray for Muslims

A Muslim-background believer in North Africa was asked, "Why do you think so many of your people are now having dreams and visions of Christ?" Her response: "I believe the prayers of people around the world have been ascending to the heavens, where they have accumulated like great monsoon clouds. Today, they are raining down upon my people miracles of grace and salvation."

(2) Support outreach and ministries to Muslims

Muslims do not come to faith in Jesus just because of a dream or vision. As it is written, "How can they believe in the one of whom they have not heard?" (Romans 10:14) Communicating the gospel to Muslims is our job. Today, there are many effective ministries to Muslims, but these require our prayerful support. We must contribute to effective outreach to Muslims.

(3) Go to Muslims

"And how can they hear without someone preaching to them?" (Romans 10:14) Some who are praying through this *30 Days Prayer Guide* are being called to take the gospel to Muslims. Unless we overcome fear and hatred, ignorance and apathy, we will be only spectators in God's great redemption story among Muslims.

(4) Minister to Muslims in your own community

Many Muslims have moved to other nations, often to flee terrors in the House of Islam or to seek a better hope for their children. How will you view Muslim immigrants to your nation? With prejudice and avoidance or as an unparalleled opportunity to share with them the love and grace of Jesus Christ?

(5) Share the gospel with Muslims

There are many ways to communicate the love and gospel of Jesus Christ effectively with Muslims. When we join in these, we catch the Wind of the Spirit that is blowing through the House of Islam and are carried along with it.

HOW CAN WE PRAY?

- *Pray for Muslims in your own community and around the world whenever they are in the news.*
- *Pray for missionaries and Muslim-background believers who are taking the gospel deep into the House of Islam.*
- *Pray that God would raise up more witnesses to Muslims, and ask God what He would have you do to minister to Muslims and share your faith with them.*

> His Spirit is drawing countless thousands of Muslims to new life in Jesus.

Prayer through the year

The Muslim Calendar is lunar based, beginning July 16, 622, when Muhammad emigrated from Mecca to Medina (this migration is known as the *hijra*). Here are some other important dates in 2015, when you can be praying:

Date	Event
June 18–July 17	Ramadan (month of fasting)
July 13	*Lailat ul-Qadr* (Night of Power)
July 17	*Id-al-Fitr* (Breaking the Fast)
September 21–26	*Hajj* (Pilgrimage to Mecca)
September 22	*Arafa* (Day to seek forgiveness)
September 23	*Id-al-Adha/Qurbani* (Festival of Sacrifice)
October 14	*Hijra* — New Year's Day
October 23	*Ashura* (Shi'ites — 10 days to commemorate the death of Husain at Karbala; Sunnis — celebrate as day of God's creation)

What now?
How will you keep praying?

Having prayed through Ramadan, consider keeping the Muslim world as a focus in your prayers throughout the year.

How do you want to see God move this next year in the life of a Muslim you know, or in a community you have prayed for?

Write it down here:

_____

_____

_____

_____

_____

_____

_____

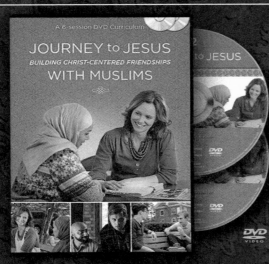

A multi-national, multi-cultural, multi-generational ministry

Praying for and Loving Muslims into God's Kingdom!
Being the fragrance of Isa Almasih (Jesus our Messiah)

LOVINGLY EMBRACING NEWCOMERS TO CANADA

Meeting felt needs and forging life-long friendships

Empowering newcomers to navigate Canadian Society

Training and equipping key individuals to bridge East and West

You are invited to PARTNER with the PALM team

Prayer
Hands on participation
Sacrificial giving

PO Box 155 Stn Main, Edmonton, AB T5J 2J1
1-780-716-0700   pmahk@shawlink.ca

Want to gain speedy access to the nations coming to Canada? Opportunities available for individuals and groups.

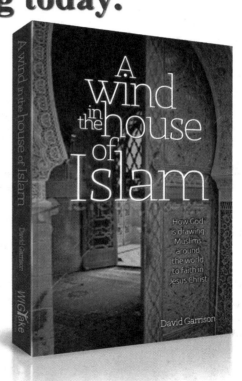

ARE YOU "N"?

Convert to Islam, pay a high tax, leave the area or die.

Those are the choices the terrorist group Islamic State (IS) gave Christians in Iraq. The group also painted the Arabic letter "N" (nun) from the word "nasara," meaning "Nazarene," on homes in Mosul to identify residents as Christians.

The Voice of the Martyrs proudly serves Christians who have fled Islamic extremism by providing them with daily necessities and assessing their future needs. You can support these Christians and stand with them by designating a contribution or purchasing one of VOM's "i-am-n" T-shirts. You can even do both. $10 from each T-shirt sale will support Christians facing Islamic extremists.

www.i-am-n.com

PRAY *for* MIRACLES
along the banks of the Ganges

"...The vast Ganges plains of North India contain the greatest concentration of un-evangelized people in the world... North India will probably be the touchstone of our success or failure in completing world evangelization in our generation. —Patrick Johnstone*"*

India is home to the third-largest population of Muslims.
This is the world's largest and most accessible community with the freedom to follow Christ!

COME JOIN US IN SPREADING THE WORD THERE!

 team

www.team.org | info@team.org | 800-343-3144

The Kelsey Arabic Program

Producing Arabic speakers for 50 years and counting.

The Kelsey Arabic Program is a two-year, four-semester, full-time program for equipping cross-cultural workers and Christian professionals in Arabic language. The program is designed to take people with no exposure or little exposure to Arabic, and after two years, have them operating with fluency in spoken Arabic, and a high level of reading comprehension in Arabic (Modern Standard/ Classical). Our locations in Amman and Madaba, Jordan and the hospitality of the Jordanian people give expats ideal settings for learning Arabic.

The Kelsey Program's comprehensive, proven methodology for Arabic learning will give you what you need to thrive and work effectively among Arabs.

With a 50-year history, the Kelsey Arabic Program has thousands of graduates around the world whose strong ability in Arabic attests to the strength of the program.

If you love Arabs, let us help you love them in their language!

Contact us today: kelseyschool@gmail.com | www.kelseyarabicprogram.org

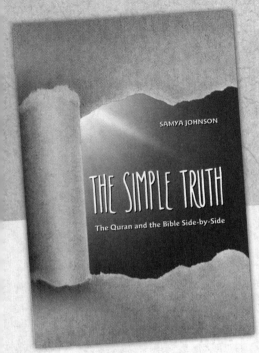

Two billion are beyond reach of the Gospel.

Let's Act Beyond.

ACT BEYOND®
MISSION : UNREACHED PEOPLES

beyond.org | actbeyond | @actbeyondupg

Disciples making disciples | Churches planting churches | Viral multiplication

DVD Resources on Islam

available from  **WORLD CHRISTIAN.COM** Resources and Ministry that Impact Our World

Loving Muslims & Sharing Jesus
A Biblical Approach to Engaging Muslims
A teaching series led by Carl Medearis and Rick Love. Over the course of eight speaking sessions, topics ranging from the basic beliefs of Muslims to learning how to effectively share Jesus with Muslims are thoroughly addressed.
*$29.99 **Sale Price: $22.49***

The Camel Rider's Journal
(DVD and Workbook)
This workshop can be completed in six one-hour sessions, taking a Christian from novice to experienced in sharing the good news of Jesus Christ with a Muslim. Born out of the largest modern movement of Muslims to Christ in the world today, the Camel method will teach you how to lovingly share in an intelligent and effective way with Muslims. (DVD and 96-page Journal) "The Camel Method is one of the most powerful Muslim evangelism tools in the world today."
Dr. Jerry Rankin, former President of the International Mission Board
*$20 **Sale Price: $17***

In the House of Islam DVD
(see description and cost on center pages)

Journey to Jesus
Building Christ-Centered Friendships with Muslims. This is a six-session two-DVD Teaching Resource that helps Christians how to reach out to Muslims in friendship with the love of Christ. Through six high-quality live-action video dramatizations and engaging teaching materials your organization, family, small group, church, or Bible study group will explore the culture and background of Muslims, as well as meet three types of Muslims (refugees or new arrivals, culturally liberal, and conservative Muslims). Includes Leader's Guide, student handouts, bonus material. *$29.99 **Sale Price: $23.99***

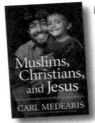

Muslims, Christians, and Jesus
Gaining Understanding and Building Relationships. According to author Carl Medearis, how Americans respond to Islam and how Christians think of Muslims could be the most significant issues of our time. With this four-session video study (includes a 92-page separate participant's guide), you will understand the basics of Islam, the difference between "moderate" Muslims and radical terrorists, the Muslim view of Jesus, and how we as Christians should interact with our Muslim neighbors, friends, and coworkers.
*$26.99 **Sale Price: $21.59***

Order these resources online at www.**WorldChristian.com** or see the order form on page 56.

Order Form

Order additional booklets for yourself or others

ADULT VERSION:	1–9 booklets: $3 each	10–49: $2.25 each	50–249: $1.75 each
KIDS VERSION:	1–9 booklets: $3.50 each	10–49: $3 each	50–249: $2.25 each

BILLING ADDRESS

Name

Address

City   State   Zip

My Phone

My Email

☐ My check is enclosed payable to WorldChristian.com
(U.S. funds, drawn on U.S. bank)

☐ Please charge my   ☐ VISA   ☐ MASTERCARD   ☐ DISCOVER   ☐ AMEX

Card No   Expiry date

Signature   CVV*

*CVV security code: VISA/MC/DISC on signature panel. AMEX front above CC no.

SHIPPING ADDRESS

If different from above

Name

Address

City   State   Zip

MAIL YOUR ORDER FORM AND PAYMENT TO:

WorldChristian.com. PO Box 9208,
Colorado Springs, CO 80932 or visit
www.WorldChristian.com
Call 888.926.6397 or 719.442.6409   Monday–Thursday 10am–3pm
Email: orders@worldchristian.com

W⊕RLD CHRISTIAN.COM
Resources and Ministry that Impact Our World

56 30 Days of Prayer for the Muslim World 2015

ITEM DESCRIPTION (see resources on center pages)	PRICE	QTY	TOTAL

Shipping cost calculations may differ slightly when ordering online

SHIPPING COSTS USA ADDRESSES
For Books (see titles on center pages)
• First item: $5 (add $1.50 for each additional)
For 30 Days Booklets
• First booklet: $2.50 (add $0.50 for each additional—up to 20)
• 20 items: $12 (add $0.20 for each additional booklet—up to 100)
• 100 items: $28 (add $0.10 for each additional booklet)

SHIPPING COSTS CANADA ADDRESSES
For Books (see titles on center pages)
• First item: $9.50 (add $3.50 for each additional)
For 30 Days Booklets
• First item: $3.00 (add $0.95 for each additional—up to 20)
• 20 items: $20 (add $0.50 for each additional booklet)

Sub Total $ _____

Sales Tax $ _____
Applies to Colorado only: 2.9%
Colorado Springs: 7.63%

Shipping & Handling $ _____

*Donation $ _____

Total $ _____

* Help us support ministry opportunities around the world. *

Your donation helps us support many small ministry initiatives. Any donation of $25 or more will receive a tax-deductible receipt from WorldChristian Concern. You can also securely donate online at www.WorldChristianConcern.org/donate